D1411383

MATH IN 30 SECONDS

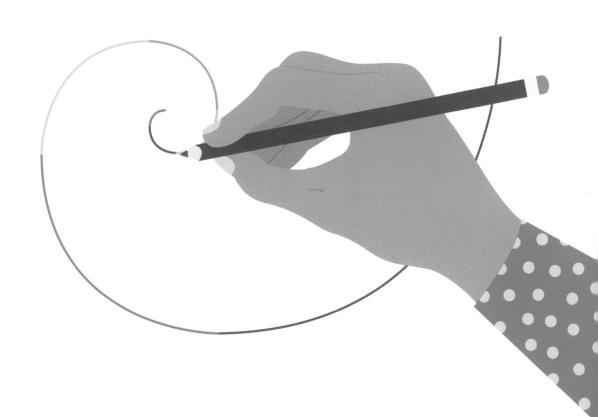

First published in the UK in 2017 by Ivy Kids.
This edition published in the US in 2017 by

Ivy Kids

An imprint of The Quarto Group
The Old Brewery
6 Blundell Street
London N7 9BH
United Kingdom
www.QuartoKnows.com

Copyright © 2017 Quarto Publishing plc

All rights reserved. No part of this book may
be reproduced or transmitted in any form or by
any means, electronic or mechanical, including
photocopying, recording, or by any information
storage-and-retrieval system, without written
permission from the copyright holder.

ISBN: 978-1-78240-530-6

This book was conceived, designed & produced by

Ivy Kids

58 West Street, Brighton BN1 2RA, United Kingdom

PUBLISHER	Susan Kelly
CREATIVE DIRECTOR	Michael Whitehead
COMMISSIONING EDITOR	Hazel Songhurst
MANAGING EDITOR	Susie Behar
PROJECT EDITOR	Leah Willey
ART DIRECTOR	Hanri van Wyk
IN-HOUSE DESIGNER	Kate Haynes
DESIGNER	Claire Munday
EDITORIAL ASSISTANT	Lucy Menzies

Printed in China

10 9 8 7 6 5 4 3 2 1

MATH
IN 30 SECONDS

ANNE ROONEY

ILLUSTRATED BY PUTRI FEBRIANA
CONSULTANT: DR. KATIE STECKLES

IVY KIDS

Contents

About this book

... in 60 seconds

You probably can't remember a time before you could count—most of us learn counting when we're very young and use numbers every day without even thinking about it. But counting is only the start! We can do lots and lots of different and amazing things with math.

Math is not just a subject you study in school. The rules of math lie behind space rockets getting to the Moon, buildings being safely constructed, every computer game you've ever played, and even the pattern on your drapes.

Math can be found in the natural world, too. Lots of things in nature are organized in ways that we can describe using numbers and shapes. The way rivers twist and galaxies spiral, the growth of tree branches, and the orbits of planets all follow mathematical patterns.

There are many ways of doing math. At various times in history and in various places across the world, people have done things differently. Our way of doing math is just one way that works. If we ever meet aliens from another planet, they might do math, too, but probably in a whole new way. Their way could work just as well!

This book reveals some of the incredible things we can do with math. You will discover a variety of ways that math helps us to explore and explain the world around us. How can math help you make decisions or predict what will happen? Are there enough numbers in the world to count all of the stars? Can we measure a volcanic eruption? Can we ever use math without using numbers? Is there more than one way to count? You can think about all these questions and many more as you read.

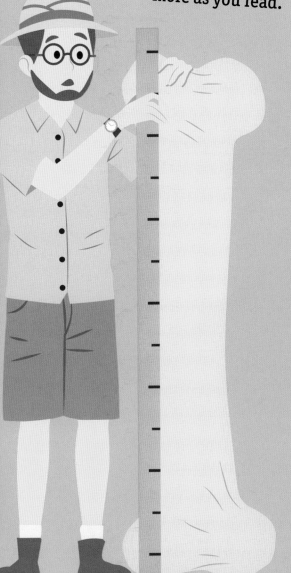

In this book, every topic has a page to read as fast as you like to grasp the main facts. If you are in a real hurry, you can read the speedy 3-second sum-up instead. Each full-page illustration gives you a colorful at-a-glance guide, too. Then, if you have a few spare minutes, there are extra facts to discover and exciting hands-on activities to try.

One, two, three, more

We use numbers every day, to count, measure, and calculate. But where do numbers come from? Can you imagine what life would be like without them? Numbers are really useful—but they can also be useless. It's possible to write a number so large that it doesn't relate to anything in the whole universe!

One, two, three, more
Glossary

area The size of a surface.

calculate To figure out using mathematical operations (adding, subtracting, multiplying, and dividing).

compare To look for similarity or difference between two or more items or sets.

decimal number A type of **fraction** that breaks numbers down into tenths, hundredths, thousandths, and so on. The whole number is separated from the fraction with a decimal point. Examples of decimal numbers include 0.1 and 2.5.

digit A symbol used to make up a **numeral**. 0, 1, 2, 3, 4, 5, 6, 7, 8, and 9 are the ten digits that we use to make numerals.

equal The same amount or **value**.

fraction Only part of a whole item or number. Fractions are helpful for counting and **measuring** between whole numbers and for splitting things into **portions** or groups. Examples of fractions include ½ and ¾.

infinite Something that goes on and on forever, having no end or limit.

measure To find out size or quantity. For example, you can measure distance, weight, volume, time, or temperature.

numeral A symbol or group of symbols representing a number.

place-value system A number system where the position of the **digits** tells us their **value**.

portion A part of a whole.

predict To state what you think will happen in the future.

tally To match one thing to another so that you can keep track.

unequal Not the same amount or **value**.

unit Another way of saying "one."

value An amount, or how much something is worth.

Where does math come from?

Humans use math to explain and predict all kinds of things. For example, people can use math to figure out the orbit of a planet or whether or not a bridge will collapse.

As far as we know, we are the first creatures on Earth to use math to do sums, create buildings, make art, and explore science, and we've only been doing it for a few thousand years. Did all of this math exist before humans started using it or did humans invent it as a way to explain the world? No one really knows.

We tend to think that the rules of math are fixed and real. We can multiply two sides of a square to find its area and the calculation works the same way every time. But in the time of the dinosaurs, no one was figuring out the area of a square, so it's hard to know if the rule existed then or not.

Although some animals do seem to have a sense of numbers (they can tell if some of their young are missing), we don't know of any animals that can use math in the way that we do.

Human laws of math might not be the only way of describing how things work. Maybe, far away, aliens have come up with a completely different kind of math that explains things in another way.

3-second sum-up

Math might exist even if there were no people—or people might have made it up.

Around and around

Long ago, people thought the Sun went around the Earth. Now scientists know the mathematical rules that explain how the planets move around the Sun. We can now predict the positions of the planets at any point in the future using math.

We use math to explain the world around us, but no one knows for sure whether we invented or discovered the laws of math.

Forms of math can be found in nature. Birds can't count like humans can, but some types of bird know if a chick is missing from the nest.

Humans use math to understand all sorts of things, such as whether a tower will fall over.

Tallying and counting

... in 30 seconds

Before people began to count in the way that we do today, they used tallies. A tally matches one object to another so that you can keep track of amounts. So, for example, one form of tallying would be a caveman making a mark on a bone for every mammoth he killed.

Similarly, if a shepherd had a stone for each sheep that he owned, and he put the stones in a pot one by one as each animal came in at night, he would be able see if any sheep were missing—there would be stones left over. But he wouldn't be able to say how many were missing unless he counted the stones.

Tallying is still useful today. We sometimes use tallies to keep the score in games, and counting on our fingers is a form of tallying, too—each finger represents one item. But it's easier if you can count.

Counting gives names to numbers. Then you can say, "three stones left," and look until you find three sheep. Counting lets us work with larger amounts, share number information with other people, make comparisons, and trade with one another.

3-second sum-up

Before people counted with numbers, they used tallies to keep track of amounts.

3-minute mission Keeping score

You need: • Paper • Pencil

Try keeping a tally. You could tally the birds you see outside the window, the cars that go past, or even how many times you hiccup! Draw a stroke for each bird, car, or hiccup up to four, then cross through the group for five and start again.

Tallies match one item to another so you can keep track of amounts, but you can do much more when you count with numbers.

A shepherd keeping track of his sheep using a tally would have one stone for each sheep.

Counting means we can be more precise. Instead of saying, "I'll give you these fish for those onions," people can count exact amounts.

Number systems

... in 30 seconds

Numerals are the squiggles (or symbols) that we write down instead of writing out the words for each number in full. The way that we show numbers using numerals is called our number system.

In our number system, we can write any numeral, even billions or trillions, using only ten different squiggles—the digits 0, 1, 2, 3, 4, 5, 6, 7, 8, and 9. We can do this because our number system is a place-value system. This means that the position of each digit in the numeral tells us its value—how many it is worth.

In any numeral, the last digit (on the right) is the number of ones (1s), or units, so it's just itself. Next on the left is the number of tens (10s), and then the number of hundreds (100s), and so on, multiplying by 10 each time. So the number 4,139 means $(4 \times 1,000) + (1 \times 100) + (3 \times 10) + (9 \times 1)$. This means we can add numbers together by lining them up above each other and adding each column.

The ancient Romans had a much harder time with their number system. They used letters to make numerals instead of digits. The letters were usually arranged from largest to smallest and added together to get the total (so LXXVII = 50 + 10 + 10 + 5 + 1 + 1 = 77). Sometimes a smaller number appeared in front of a larger one, meaning it had to be taken away. So 4 was written IV (5—1) and 90 was written XC (100—10). Numbers could get very long!

3-second sum-up

Our number system is a place-value system—the place of a digit shows its value.

3-minute mission Make a Roman calendar

You need: • Paper • Pencil • Markers or colored pencils • Or an art program on the computer

Most of the names for the days and months have ancient Roman roots. Make an ancient Roman calendar for the current month, using Roman numerals for the dates. You can do it on the computer or on paper. Decorate your calendar.

In our place-value number system, we only use the digits 0-9.
The ancient Romans used letters as digits.

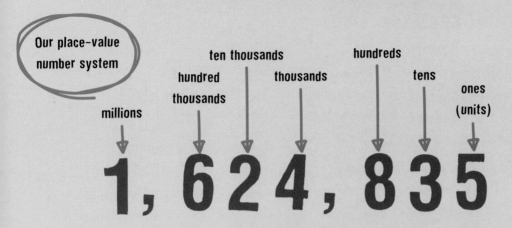

Our place-value number system

millions | hundred thousands | ten thousands | thousands | hundreds | tens | ones (units)

1, 624, 835

Roman numeral number system

I	II	III	IV	V	VI	VII	VIII	IX	X
1	2	3	4	5	6	7	8	9	10
XI	XII	XIII	XIV	XV	XVI	XVII	XVIII	XIX	XX
11	12	13	14	15	16	17	18	19	20

XL	L	LX	XC	XCIX	C	D	M
40	50	60	90	99	100	500	1,000

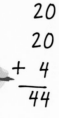

```
  20
  20
+  4
----
  44
```

It's easy to do calculations in a place-value system if you line the numbers up above each other. This wasn't so easy for the ancient Romans!

XX + XX + IV =

Base 10

... in 30 seconds

If you were an octopus, do you think you would count in the same way as humans do? Humans use a number system based on 10 because we have 10 fingers. If an octopus could count, maybe it would have a number system based on 8 instead.

We call our number system "base 10" because we start reusing our digits after 9, when we get to 10. Our place-value system uses 10 to show one ten and no units.

An octopus counting in base 8 would count up to 7 and then use 10 to show one eight and no units. Counting in bases of less than ten means some of our digits are never used. Base 8 has no use for the digits 8 or 9.

A number system based on 2 is called a binary system. It uses only 0 and 1, starting again with 10 where we have 2. The numbers get long very quickly:

0	1	2	3	4	5	6	7	8	9	10
0	1	10	11	100	101	110	111	1000	1001	1010

3-second sum-up

10 doesn't always mean 1 more than 9—it depends which base system you're counting in.

How does a computer count?

Computers sometimes use base 16, which is called hexadecimal. Instead of being based on 10, it's based on 16. There's no single-digit way to write 10, 11, 12, 13, 14, and 15, so in hexadecimal, letters are used: 10 is written as A, 11 = B, 12 = C, and so on, up to 15 = F; then 10 in hexadecimal represents one sixteen and no units.

Our number system reuses digits after the number 9 because we have 10 fingers. But a system that restarts after the number 7, 3, or even after 1, is possible!

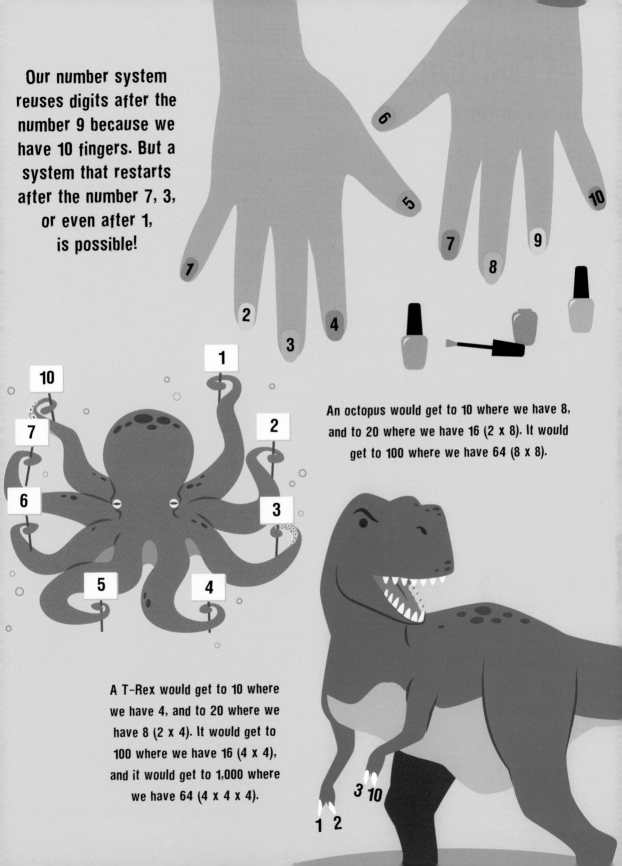

An octopus would get to 10 where we have 8, and to 20 where we have 16 (2 x 8). It would get to 100 where we have 64 (8 x 8).

A T-Rex would get to 10 where we have 4, and to 20 where we have 8 (2 x 4). It would get to 100 where we have 16 (4 x 4), and it would get to 1,000 where we have 64 (4 x 4 x 4).

Fractions

... in 30 seconds

Imagine you have a pizza to share with five friends. How much will you each get? Answer: less-than-one pizza! What if you shared it with only three friends? You'd still each get less-than-one pizza, but it would be a bigger piece each. Counting or measuring between zero and one needs a special kind of numbers—these are called fractions.

If you cut the pizza into three equal pieces, there would be three thirds. One third can be written like this—$\frac{1}{3}$—to show that it is 1 cut into (or divided by) 3. What if one friend went home without eating their piece, leaving just two of you to eat three pieces of pizza? One person could have two thirds ($\frac{2}{3}$) and the other could have one third ($\frac{1}{3}$), but that's not very fair. The best thing would be to cut the spare third in half ($\frac{1}{2}$) to make two slices. Half of one third is one sixth ($\frac{1}{6}$), so the new slices would each be one sixth of the pizza.

The calculation for this is: $\frac{1}{2} \times \frac{1}{3} = \frac{1}{6}$

You get the answer by multiplying the numbers above and below the line, like this:

$1 \times 1 = 1$

$2 \times 3 = 6.$

3-second sum-up

Using fractions lets us work with parts and pieces instead of just whole numbers.

Decimals are best

Decimals are special fractions: they break down numbers into tenths, hundredths, thousandths, and so on. We separate whole numbers from the fraction with a decimal point. So 1.0, means one and no tenths, 0.5 means zero and five tenths or $\frac{5}{10}$, and 3.7 means three and seven tenths or $3\frac{7}{10}$. It's easier to calculate with decimals than other fractions. Adding $\frac{5}{8}$ and $\frac{3}{10}$ is quite hard, but converted to decimals, it's much easier: $0.625 + 0.3 = 0.925$.

Fractions are great when you need to share. You can use them to split any item or any number of items into smaller portions.

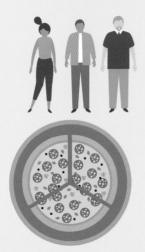

For three people sharing one pizza, you could divide it into equal thirds.

For five people sharing two pizzas, you could divide each one into equal fifths.

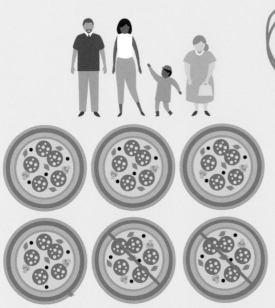

For four people sharing six smaller pizzas, you could divide two in half. Each person would get one and a half.

You can use fractions to divide things into unequal portions, too.

For two people sharing one pizza, you could divide it into unequal portions—one big piece (three quarters) and one small piece (one quarter).

Never-ending numbers

... in 30 seconds

How far can you count? In theory, you could count forever, but you would soon get very bored. If you counted all day and all night, without stopping, saying one number each second, it would take nearly 12 days to count to a million. It would take 31 years and 7 months to count to a billion!

Big numbers get fairly long to write out in full as numerals, but we can write them in a shorter way that shows how many zeros there are:

1,000 means $10 \times 10 \times 10$, so we write it as 10^3

$1,000,000 = 10^6$

$1,000,000,000 = 10^9$

We also have "illion" names, like million, billion, and trillion, for numbers up to nonillion (10^{30}), and then the "illion" names run out. But there are some special names for really big numbers. A googol is 1 followed by 100 zeros (written 10^{100}) and a googolplex is 1 followed by a googol zeros (written 10^{googol}). People haven't found anything that we could count to reach a googol, nevermind a googolplex—not even all the atoms in the universe would be enough!

3-second sum-up

Numbers never end—but words for them do!

Numbers go on and on

There is no end to numbers—they are infinite. That means they go on and on forever. You can always add just one more, no matter how far you count. You can also keep counting forever below zero using negative numbers: -1, -2 ... -4,892,543 ... and so on!

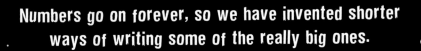

Numbers go on forever, so we have invented shorter ways of writing some of the really big ones.

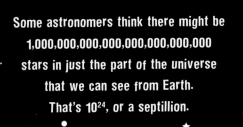

Some astronomers think there might be 1,000,000,000,000,000,000,000,000 stars in just the part of the universe that we can see from Earth. That's 10^{24}, or a septillion.

There's even more universe that we can't see and we don't know how big it is. How many stars might it have?

Super shapes

Shapes are all around you. Some are regular shapes, like squares or hexagons, and others are wiggly or jagged irregular shapes, like the shape of a puddle or a spiky leaf. Some shapes fit together or repeat themselves to make patterns. Shapes can be flat, like a piece of paper, or they can take up space, like a box or a rubber ball.

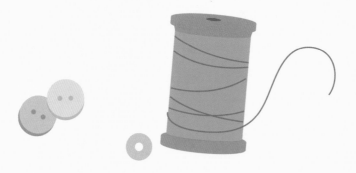

Super shapes
Glossary

area The size of a surface.

axis of symmetry A line that divides a **symmetrical** shape or object in half. If you folded a symmetrical shape along the axis of symmetry, the two halves would match.

calculate To figure out using mathematical operations (adding, subtracting, multiplying, and dividing).

dimension A measurement of the size of something in one direction. **Length**, **width**, and **height** are dimensions. A line has one dimension, a flat shape has two dimensions, and a solid object has three dimensions.

distort To pull, push, or twist out of shape.

face A flat surface of a solid shape or object.

finite Something that has a limit.

fractal A **pattern** that goes on and on repeating itself, at increasingly smaller scales.

height The distance from the bottom of a shape or object to the top.

infinite Something that goes on forever, having no end or limit.

irregular shapes Shapes that are not **regular**.

length The distance from one end of a shape or object to the other end.

measure To find out size or quantity. For example, you can measure distance, weight, **volume**, time, or temperature.

pattern A design or sequence that repeats itself.

perimeter The distance around the outside of a 2D shape.

proportion The number or size of a part of something in relation to the whole thing.

ratio The relationship between two or more items or quantities. For example, if a rectangle has one side that is 3 in long and one side that is 4 in long, the ratio of the two sides would be 3:4.

reflection A mirror image. You can see your own reflection if you look in a mirror.

regular shapes Shapes with all sides and all angles equal.

resizing Making a shape or object bigger or smaller, keeping all the **proportions** the same.

rotation Turning a shape or object around a fixed point.

surface area The total **area** of the surface of a 3D shape or object.

symmetry A shape or object is symmetrical when it looks the same after **reflection** or **rotation**.

tessellation A **pattern** made from repeating shapes that fit together to fill an **area**, without any gaps or overlapping.

transformation Changing a shape or object. **Reflection**, **rotation**, **translation**, and **resizing** are all types of transformation.

translation Moving a shape or object, without **reflection**, **rotation,** or **resizing**.

unit (of measurement) A standard quantity, such as inches, ounces, pounds, and minutes.

volume The amount of space taken up by a 3D shape or object.

width The distance from one side of a shape or object to the other side.

Dimensions

What's the difference between a circle and a sphere? Or a square and a cube? It's all about dimensions. A dimension is a measurement in a certain direction and the number of dimensions a shape has determines whether it's flat or solid.

Imagine a point—a dot like this •—but so small that you can't measure it. If you added another point and joined the two together, you would have a line. A line has length, which you can measure in one direction. This means that a line is one-dimensional.

If you added more lines and joined them together as an outline, you would have a flat shape, such as a triangle or a rectangle. You can measure a flat shape in two directions. For example, you could measure the length and the width of a rectangle, so we call flat shapes two-dimensional. You can figure out the size of the shape's surface—this is called area.

Then imagine turning your flat shape into a shape that takes up space. You could turn your triangle into a pyramid or your rectangle into a cuboid. This gives the shape a third measurable direction: we can measure the length, the width, and the height, so we call solid shapes three-dimensional. You can calculate how much space 3D shapes take up—this is called volume.

3-second sum-up

Lines are one-dimensional; shapes can be two-dimensional or three-dimensional.

3-minute mission Shapes and solids

See if you can find objects in your home or school that are these shapes: a flat square, a flat circle, and a flat rectangle. Now try to find objects that have the same flat shape at the end but are three-dimensional: a cube, a cylinder, and a cuboid.

Flat shapes have two dimensions and you can calculate their area. Solid shapes have three dimensions and you can calculate their volume.

A line has one dimension—you can measure it in one direction.

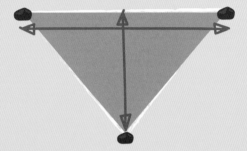

A flat shape has two dimensions—you can measure it in two directions. It has an AREA.

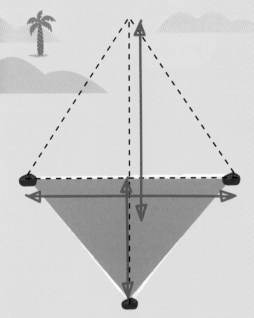

Adding another direction gives you a three-dimensional shape.

A 3D shape takes up space. It has a VOLUME.

Area and volume

... in 30 seconds

The line around a 2D shape, like the fence around a field, is called the perimeter. Its length is measured in "linear" units, such as inches or feet. You can figure out the length of a perimeter by adding together the lengths of all of the sides.

The amount of space contained within a perimeter is called the area. A field has an area. Areas are measured in "square" units, such as square inches (in^2) or square feet (ft^2). The area of a square or rectangle is easy to figure out: it's length × width. The same perimeter can enclose different areas, or the same area can be enclosed by a different perimeter, depending on the shape.

For 3D shapes, the area of all of the faces added together gives the total surface area. The space contained within the shape is called the volume. Volumes are measured in "cubic" units, such as cubic inches (in^3). You can easily figure out the volume of lots of 3D shapes. For example, the volume of a cuboid is length × width × height. Shapes with the same surface area can have different volumes, and the same volume can be contained within shapes with different surface areas.

3-second sum-up

2D shapes have a perimeter and an area. 3D shapes have a surface area and a volume.

3-minute mission Making areas

You need: • String • Graph paper

Using string, make a long, thin enclosed shape on top of the graph paper. Count the squares inside it. Using the same piece of string, make other shapes. Count the squares. Which shape encloses the largest area? The perimeter is the same, but the area is different!

Surface-area-to-volume ratio

... in 30 seconds

Did you know that a long, thin shape always has a larger surface area than a short, wide shape that has the same volume? The relationship between the outside area of a solid shape and its volume (the amount of space it takes up) is called the surface-area-to-volume ratio. A ratio tells you how much of one thing there is compared to another.

For animals, a higher surface-area-to-volume ratio makes it harder to stay the same temperature. The hot sun or cold wind acts on the animal's surface—its skin. A small mouse gets cold more quickly than a large dog or an elephant because it has more in^2 of outside (its skin) for each in^3 of inside.

It may sound strange, but a small, chocolate-covered candy—such as a chocolate raisin—would taste more chocolatey than a larger version of the same candy. The small candy has less total chocolate, but proportionally more chocolate compared to the filling—it has a higher surface-area-to-volume ratio.

3-second sum-up

Squat, solid shapes have a lower surface-area-to-volume ratio than stretched or flattened shapes.

3-minute mission Surface area and speed

You need: • Scales • Sugar cubes • Loose sugar • Two cups of hot water • An adult helper

Weigh two sugar cubes. Now weigh out the same amount of loose sugar. Pour two identical cups of hot water. Put the loose sugar into one cup and the sugar cubes into the other. Which dissolves first?

Answer on page 96

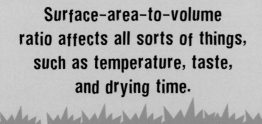

Surface-area-to-volume ratio affects all sorts of things, such as temperature, taste, and drying time.

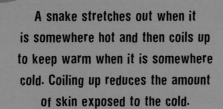

A snake stretches out when it is somewhere hot and then coils up to keep warm when it is somewhere cold. Coiling up reduces the amount of skin exposed to the cold.

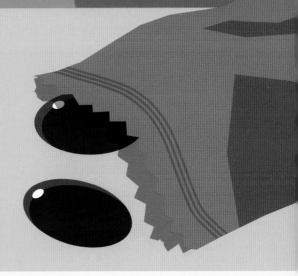

There is a higher surface-area-to-volume ratio in the smaller candy. This means it tastes more chocolatey than the bigger one—even though it actually has less chocolate!

Water evaporates faster from a larger surface area, so your wet bathing suit dries more quickly spread out than it will if left in a pile.

Strong shapes
... in 30 seconds

Humans make lots of 3D objects, and many of them need to be strong. This strength comes partially from the material that things are made from, and partially from their shape.

Suppose an elephant went rampaging through a village, bashing into buildings and other structures. Which shapes would be strongest? Although most modern buildings are square or rectangular, those are not really the strongest shapes. We make rectangular buildings because the shape is convenient in other ways. But triangles, hexagons, and even circles are actually stronger, as they are harder to distort.

If you look carefully, you'll see that there are quite a few triangles found in buildings. Roofs have triangular supports. Many very tall buildings are wider at the base and get narrower at the top. This makes them less likely to fall over.

Bridges are rarely a flat piece of road stretched between two banks: they often have arches. Arches are strong because the weight pressing from the top of the bridge holds the stones in place. Wedge-shaped bricks can't fall downward as there isn't room for them to squeeze past each other—they just press closer together.

3-second sum-up

The strength of a 3D object partially depends on the shapes used to build it.

3-minute mission Bending and breaking

You need: • Cardboard • Scissors • Adhesive tape

Use strips of cardboard to make some shapes: a triangle, a square, and an arch. How easy is it to push each of them out of shape?

Some shapes are stronger than others.

Arches make strong structures.
The bricks are wider at the top than
the bottom, so they can't fall downward
under pressure from above.

A flat surface supported only
at the edges is not a strong
structure. Pressure in the middle
can make it give way.

An igloo is strong because
pushing on the top just pushes
the blocks of ice closer together.
The middle can't fall down as it's
resting on the sides.

Fractal patterns

... in 30 seconds

Have you ever noticed how some patterns break down into smaller and smaller copies of themselves? A tree trunk splits into branches, which then split into smaller branches, which then split again, right down to thin twigs. This type of pattern, which can go on and on repeating itself at increasingly smaller scales, is called a fractal.

Tree branches and roots form a pattern that spreads out from a single line, but some fractal patterns can enclose an area. An example of this is the "Koch snowflake" (see the mission box below). The perimeter of a fractal that is a closed shape gets longer and longer the more the pattern repeats. Every time more wiggles and corners are added to the line, the total outline gets larger.

But the area inside the shape can't grow beyond a certain size because the first points are fixed. This leads to a crazy-sounding result. The outline of the shape is infinite, because it can continue getting longer forever. But the area within the outline is finite (limited). The area can never get larger than a circle drawn around the shape right at the beginning.

3-second sum-up

A fractal is a pattern that repeats again and again, getting smaller each time.

3-minute mission Draw a fractal

You need: • Paper • Ruler • Pencil • Eraser

Draw an equilateral triangle. Now divide each side into three equal sections. Draw an equilateral triangle above the middle section on each side and erase the lines where the new triangles join the old one. Repeat the process with each new triangle. Keep going as long as you can. The fractal you've drawn is called a "Koch snowflake."

You can see lots of examples of repeating fractal patterns in nature.

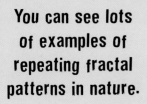

It's hard to see lightning clearly since it goes so quickly—but its forking forms fractal patterns.

Streams flowing down perfectly smooth mountains would probably form fractals—but in reality, rocks and dirt get in the way.

Tree branches often form fractal patterns—and the same happens underground in the roots.

Fern plants are fractals. Each plant is divided into leaves. Each leaf is divided in the same pattern as the plant. Each subleaf is split into even smaller versions of the same shape.

Transformations

... in 30 seconds

In a mirror, your reflection shows your features switched from one side of your body to the other. If you had a scratch on your right knee, it would be on the left knee of your reflection. Reflection is one of the ways that we can transform a shape or image. It's the same as flipping it over. It can be reflected top-to-bottom or left-to-right.

There are many other ways we can transform shapes, including rotation, translation, and resizing. Whenever a shape is reflected, rotated, or translated, it stays the same size and shape.

Rotating something means turning it around. Pick one point, which will stay still, and turn the shape or object around that point. If you turn it all the way around, back to where it started, it will look exactly the same. Translating an object means moving it—like sliding it along a table.

Resizing a shape makes it bigger or smaller, but it keeps all the same proportions. It's like looking through a magnifying glass or the wrong end of a telescope (which makes things look smaller).

3-second sum-up

Reflection, rotation, and translation move shapes without changing their size. Resizing makes things bigger or smaller.

3-minute mission Zooming in

You need: • A picture • Ruler • Pencil • Paper

Draw a grid over the picture. Draw a grid of larger squares on another piece of paper. To double the size of the picture, make the new squares twice as big. Carefully copy the contents of each small square into each matching large square. The picture will be just the same—but bigger!

To transform a shape or image, you can rotate it, reflect it, translate it, or resize it.

To rotate an object, turn it around a pivot point. Its size and shape remain the same, it's just moved around.

A reflection is a mirror image. The object keeps all the same shapes and lines, it's just flipped over.

Translation moves the object to a new position. It doesn't change in any other way.

The shape and proportions stay the same when an object is resized, but it gets bigger or smaller.

Symmetry

... in 30 seconds

Look at yourself in the mirror. See how your left half and right half roughly match? One side of you is a reflection of the other side. If you could fold yourself in half, your left half would pretty much cover your right half, with no gaps or overlaps. That's because you are almost symmetrical.

If you drew an imaginary line dividing your body in half vertically through your nose and your belly button, you would be symmetrical around that line. This line is called an "axis of symmetry."

Symmetrical shapes repeat themselves on either side of an axis of symmetry. Some shapes have more than one axis of symmetry—they could be folded in more than one direction and have no overlaps or gaps. A rectangle has two axes of symmetry, and a square has four—you could fold it top-to-bottom or left-to-right, or diagonally in either direction.

A circle can be folded in half at any point, so it has an infinite, or endless, number of axes of symmetry. A shape that looks the same when you rotate it, a star for example, has rotational symmetry.

3-second sum-up

Symmetrical shapes are made of matching, facing parts placed around one or more axes.

3-minute mission Make a mask

You need: • Paper • Pencil • Scissors • Colored felt or foam • Markers • Twine or elastic cord

Fold the paper in half and draw one side of an animal or monster face with the fold going down the middle. Cut around the outline, leaving the fold intact. Unfold the symmetrical face and lay it on the felt or foam, then cut around it. Decorate it. Make holes on either side and attach elastic cord or twine.

Shapes can have more than one axis of symmetry.

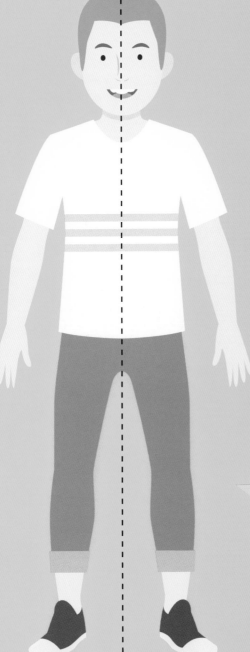

This triangle has one axis of symmetry.

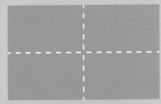

A rectangle has two axes of symmetry.

A square has four axes of symmetry.

A circle has infinite axes of symmetry.

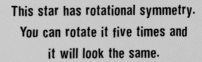

This star has rotational symmetry. You can rotate it five times and it will look the same.

Most animals are roughly symmetrical around one axis, like you.

Tessellations

... in 30 seconds

Wrapping paper, wallpaper, and fabric can have lots of different patterns: stripes, polka dots, flowers, superheroes, cars, dinosaurs, fairies ... But if you look closely, you'll see that the design is often actually a picture drawn in a square, rectangle, hexagon, or triangle and repeated again and again. It might be transformed—rotated or reflected, for instance—but it's the same picture each time.

M.C. Escher

Shapes that completely fill an area without leaving any gaps are said to "tessellate." It's easy to cover an area with repeating squares or rectangles. That's why most floor and wall tiles are square or rectangular. Hexagons and some triangles also tessellate. Circles don't tessellate—there are always little gaps between them.

It's possible to draw tessellating patterns based on different shapes. The artist M.C. Escher made lots of pictures by drawing unusual tessellations. He drew animal shapes, such as lizards, bats, or birds, that fit together perfectly.

3-second sum-up

Tessellating shapes fit neatly together without any gaps.

3-minute mission Design your own wallpaper

You need: • Paper • Ruler • Pencil • Scissors • Markers or colored pencils • Or an art program on the computer

Choose a shape that will tessellate and draw a design inside it. Make lots of copies of the shape with your design on it and fit them all together to make a repeating pattern. You can do it on the computer, or draw one and then scan it. Or you can do it all on paper if you prefer.

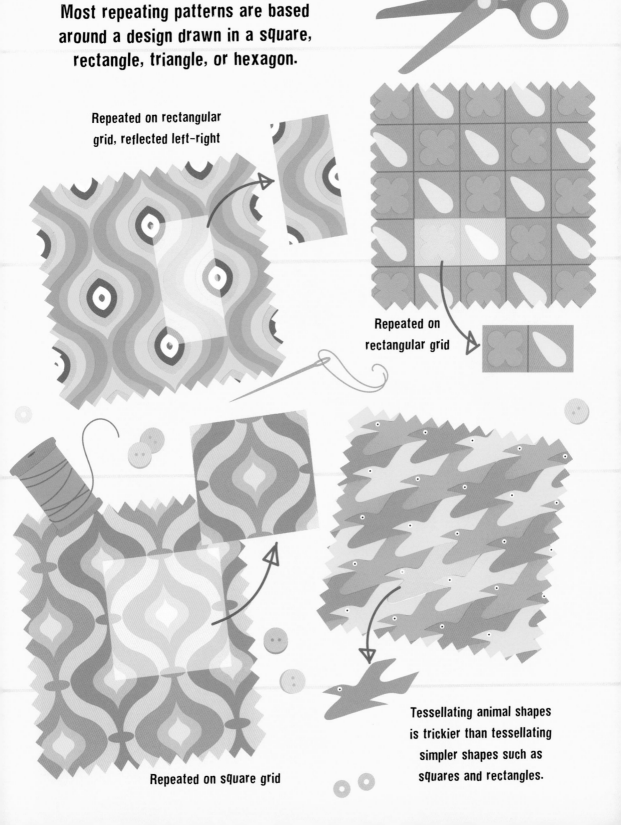

Most repeating patterns are based around a design drawn in a square, rectangle, triangle, or hexagon.

Repeated on rectangular grid, reflected left-right

Repeated on rectangular grid

Repeated on square grid

Tessellating animal shapes is trickier than tessellating simpler shapes such as squares and rectangles.

Numbers in nature

Math is everywhere in the natural world and there are certain numbers, shapes, and patterns that appear in nature again and again. Nature likes circles, curves, and spirals most of all. You can see them in round fruit and flowers, snails' shells, and galaxies, winding rivers, spreading ripples, and arching rainbows. Natural things make these shapes without knowing any math—and they were doing this long before we were around to figure out the math behind the shapes and patterns.

Numbers in nature
Glossary

area The size of a surface.

circumference The distance around the outside of a circle. The circumference is another word for the **perimeter** of a circle.

diameter A straight line going across a circle from one side to the other, through the center.

Fibonacci sequence A sequence of numbers named after the Italian mathematician, Fibonacci. Every number in the sequence is the sum of the two numbers before it. It starts like this: 0, 1, 1, 2, 3, 5, 8, 13, 21, 34 ...

golden rectangle A rectangle that has sides roughly in the **ratio** 1:1.62. The golden rectangle is often seen in art and architecture.

golden spiral A spiral that is based on the **ratio** 1:1.62.

pattern A design or **sequence** that repeats itself.

perimeter The distance around the outside of a 2D shape.

pi (π) A special number (roughly 3.142) that defines how circles work. The **circumference** of a circle is always equal to the **diameter** multiplied by pi and the **area** of a circle is always equal to pi multiplied by the **radius squared**.

radius A straight line going from the center of a circle to the **circumference**. The radius is half of the **diameter**.

ratio The relationship between two or more items or quantities. For example, if a rectangle has one side that is 3 in long and one side that is 4 in long, the ratio of the two sides would be 3:4.

sequence A set of numbers or shapes presented in a particular order.

squared Multiplied by itself.

A piece of pi

... in 30 seconds

The natural world is full of circles and curves. A circle has been called the perfect shape. A circle is the best shape for fitting the most area inside an outline, it doesn't have any weak points, and every point on the outline is the same distance from the center as every other point.

The perimeter of a circle is called the circumference. A line drawn across the circle from one side to the other, going through the middle, is called the diameter. It's the same length wherever you draw it. Half the diameter is called the radius.

There's something very strange about circles. The circumference is always equal to the diameter multiplied by a special number, called pi. The symbol for pi is π. Pi is about 3.142, or about $^{22}/_7$. It was discovered at least 4,000 years ago. The area of a circle is always pi × radius × radius (written πr^2).

What's really interesting is that pi turns up elsewhere in nature, too—it's not just a number we use to explain circles. If you measured the actual lengths of a lot of rivers (right from where they start, all the way to the ocean), and then you measured the distance that the rivers cover as straight lines (from their starting points to the ocean), the average of wiggly-distance divided by straight-distance would be pi.

3-second sum-up

The circumference of a circle is always equal to the diameter multiplied by pi.

3-minute mission Celebrate Pi Day with a pie!

You need: • A circular pie • String • Ruler

Pi Day is on March 14 because the date is written 3.14, just like pi! Cut a piece of string to fit exactly around the outside of your pie. Measure the string. Measure across the middle of the pie. Divide the length of the string by the diameter of the pie. The answer is pi! Now you can eat the pie.

Circles are everywhere—especially in nature—and they're always defined by pi.

circumference

diameter

radius

You can figure out the circumference and the area of any circle using the diameter, the radius, and pi.

circumference = diameter × π

area = π × radius²

Fibonacci's sequence

... in 30 seconds

If you had two pet rabbits, a boy and a girl, it's likely that you'd have quite a few more rabbits after a short time. Rabbit populations grow quickly. The Italian mathematician Fibonacci noticed this around 800 years ago. He began to think about how quickly the rabbits would build up if he left them alone to breed.

Fibonacci
(born around 1170)

He figured out that if you started with two rabbits (one pair), and each month they produced another pair, and none of the rabbits ever died, the number would increase in a pattern. He assumed that it takes a month for each pair to grow up and then another month to have their own babies. Each adult pair then has a pair of babies each month.

Soon, the place would be flooded with rabbits! The pattern Fibonacci found can be seen elsewhere in nature and is called the Fibonacci sequence. It's easy to figure out the next number in Fibonacci's sequence—just add the previous two numbers together:

0	1	1	2	3	5	8	13	21	34
		=0+1	=1+1	=1+2	=2+3	=3+5	=5+8	=8+13	=13+21

3-second sum-up

The Fibonacci sequence shows how things multiply if they keep reproducing: 0, 1, 1, 2, 3, 5, 8, 13 ...

3-minute mission Flower power

Many flowers have a Fibonacci number of petals, such as 3, 5, or 8. Next time you visit a nursery, park, or garden, see how many different flowers you can find with a Fibonacci number of petals. How far up can you go? Can you find any with 13 or 21 petals?

The Fibonacci sequence occurs repeatedly in the natural world.

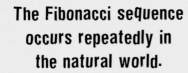

Fibonacci noticed that there was a pattern in the way that rabbit populations grew.

Baby

Adult

December	1 pair
January	1 pair
February	2 pairs
March	3 pairs
April	5 pairs
May	8 pairs

Many trees develop following the Fibonacci sequence. As the trunk and branches grow, they split into two at regular stages, right to the ends of the smallest twigs.

13 branches

8 branches

5 branches

3 branches

2 branches

1 trunk

Golden shapes

... in 30 seconds

Do you have a favorite shape? Nature seems to have a favorite, as there's one shape that appears all over the natural world: the spiral. Another shape, called the golden rectangle, seems to be a favorite with humans. It often turns up in art and architecture made by people.

A golden rectangle has sides roughly in the ratio 1:1.62. That means that if the short sides are each 1 foot long, the long sides must be about 1.62 feet long. Any rectangle with these proportions has a very special feature: if you cut a square off the end, the left-over smaller rectangle is also a golden rectangle (see opposite). You can keep on doing this, getting smaller and smaller golden rectangles each time.

Many things in nature form spirals. It's a simple way to grow, getting larger by just adding a bit more to the outside. Pineapples and fir cones have nodules arranged in spirals, the seeds in sunflower heads are arranged in a spiral, and hurricanes and some galaxies form spirals, too. You can draw a special type of spiral from the golden rectangle. It's called a golden spiral. Draw smaller and smaller golden rectangles, cutting off squares each time, then draw a curved line through the opposite corners of the squares to make a spiral (see opposite).

3-second sum-up

The golden rectangle and the golden spiral are fascinating shapes defined by the ratio 1:1.62.

3-minute mission A golden temple

You need: • Wooden or plastic construction blocks • Ruler • Calculator

Using the ruler and the calculator to get the measurements right, design a building based around golden rectangles and then try to build it. Each rectangle must have long sides that are 1.6 times the length of the short sides. You might not be able to get it perfect because of the size of your bricks— but do the best you can!

Spirals and the golden rectangle crop up all over the place, in nature and in things made by humans.

Lots of things grow in spirals, including snails' shells, galaxies, and parts of many plants.

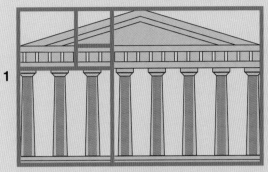

1

1.62

Golden rectangles are frequently used in art and architecture, from ancient Greek temples to modern paintings. They always have sides roughly in the ratio 1:1.62.

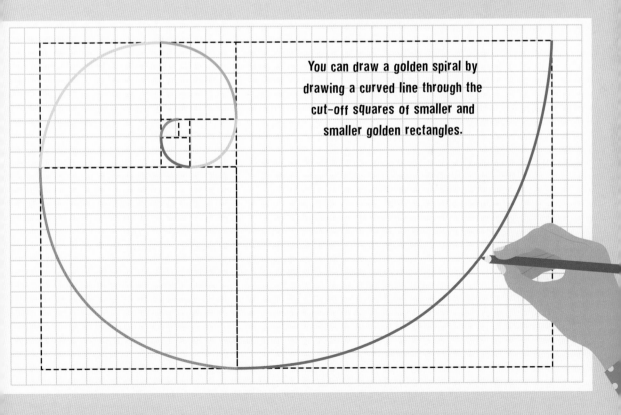

You can draw a golden spiral by drawing a curved line through the cut-off squares of smaller and smaller golden rectangles.

Measuring

We can't count everything—we can't count an amount of water or how heavy some butter is. When we can't count, we measure instead. Different units of measurement are used for measuring different types of things. So, for example, we don't measure the size of an ant in the same way that we measure how hot it is outside on a sunny day, and we don't measure an ant using the same units that we use to measure the distance to the sun.

Measuring
Glossary

area The size of a surface.

calculate To figure out using mathematical operations (adding, subtracting, multiplying, and dividing).

depth The **distance** from the top of an object to the bottom.

dimension A **measurement** of the size of something in one direction. **Length**, height, and width are dimensions. A line has one dimension, a flat shape has two dimensions, and a solid object has three dimensions.

distance The **length** between two points or objects.

length The **distance** from one end of a shape or object to the other end.

measure To find out size or quantity. For example, you can measure **distance**, weight, **volume**, time, or temperature.

quantity How much of something there is.

ratio The relationship between two or more items or **quantities**. For example, if a rectangle has one side that is 3 in long and one side that is 4 in long, the ratio of the two sides would be 3:4.

relative Looking at something in relation to something else.

standardized Something that is widely accepted and agreed upon.

surface area The total **area** of the surface of a 3D shape or object.

unit (of measurement) A standard **quantity**, such as inches, ounces, pounds, and minutes.

volume The amount of space taken up by a solid shape or object.

Counting or measuring?

... in 30 seconds

It's easy to count separate things of a reasonable size—cows, say, or toy cars. But some things are really too small to count. For example, you wouldn't want to count the number of grains of rice you had with your dinner. And then there are some things that can't be counted—you can't count the water in your cup or the length of a piece of string.

When we can't count something, we can usually measure it instead. We can measure distances, such as how long, high, or wide something is. We can measure volumes, such as how much water is in a bucket.

There are lots of things to measure. For example, we can measure weight or mass (how heavy something is), temperature (how hot something is), and time (how long something takes). We can even measure things you wouldn't really think about, such as how loud a sound is or how bright a star is.

3-second sum-up

We measure the things that we can't count.

3-minute mission Measure your lungs

You need: • Large bowl • Measuring cup • Water • Balloon

1 Put the bowl in the sink. Using the cup, measure how much water it takes to fill the bowl to the top.

2 Take a big breath, then blow all of the air out into the balloon.

3 Tie off the balloon and push it completely under the water, trying to keep your fingers out of the water as much as you can. Some water will splash out.

4 Measure the water left in the bowl. The difference between the measurements is the volume of your breath.

For things like time, temperature, volume, and weight, we can't count amounts so we measure them instead.

Oven temperature is shown in degrees.

We measure time in hours, minutes, and seconds—or days, weeks, and years.

We can't count milk, so we check the volume in cups or pints.

We can't count flour or butter, so we weigh them in ounces or pounds.

Eggs are easy to count since they are separate objects.

Units of measurement

... in 30 seconds

Can you measure a tiny insect the same way you can measure a galaxy? Not quite! We need different units of measurement for different scales.

You might measure a tiny insect in fractions of inches (in), your height in feet (ft), the length of a soccer field in yards (y), and the distance to school in miles (m).

Even miles aren't big enough for measurements in space. The Sun is about 93 million miles away from the Earth—but the next-closest star system, Alpha Centauri, is about 275,000 times as far away. That's more than 25 trillion miles. Luckily, there's a special way of measuring distances in space: light-years.

A light-year is the distance light travels in a year. Light travels at the speed of light (of course!); that's 186,000 miles a second—so it goes a long way in a year. Alpha Centauri is nearly 4½ light-years away. The Sun is only eight light-minutes away—this means that it takes eight minutes for sunlight to reach the Earth.

3-second sum-up

We need units of measurement at different scales, so that we can measure from tiny to huge.

Biggest and smallest

The very smallest unit of measurement for distance is the Planck length. It's about 0.00000000000000000000000000000000062 992 of an inch and is used for describing lengths smaller than the parts of an atom.

At the other end of the scale, a "gigaparsec" is 3.26 billion light-years. That's about one fourteenth of the distance from here to the edge of the visible universe.

It wouldn't work to use the same unit of measurement for everything, so we have lots of different ones.

We can measure larger animals in feet or yards.

Scientists measure tiny creatures in fractions of inches, centimeters, and millimeters.

Short running races are measured in yards. If you could run at the speed of light, you could go all around the Earth 7.5 times in one second!

The distances between stars are measured in light-years. A light-year is nearly 6 trillion miles.

Agreed measurements
... in 30 seconds

Sometimes we need to measure things precisely, but at other times, we can be less exact. For example, you would probably measure your height to be accurate to an inch, but you just wouldn't be able to measure the distance to school as precisely. For a start, you would need to pinpoint a small, exact spot to count as "at school" and another equally specific spot to count as "at home." So, in this case, it is generally agreed that a less accurate measurement is good enough.

We also have to agree on the measurements we use. There's no point measuring distances in paces or feet and not saying whose pace or foot we are using, so measurements are standardized. There is an agreed length that is a foot, an agreed volume that is a gallon, and an agreed change in temperature that is a degree Fahrenheit.

Humans didn't make up all the measurements we use. The Earth goes around the Sun once in a year, and rotates once in a day. Years and days are called "absolute" measures; they would be the same even if there were no people. But hours, minutes, and seconds are the measurements we have chosen to divide days by.

3-second sum-up

We use agreed units of measurement to keep a sensible level of accuracy.

3-minute mission Your body in numbers

You need: • Pencil • Paper • Tape measure and ruler

Draw a picture of yourself. Then measure: your height; around your waist; around your wrist; the length of your leg; across your smallest fingernail; your nose; a hair from your head. Write the measurements on the picture.

Which have you measured in feet, which in inches, and which in fractions of an inch?

Answers on page 96

Some agreed measurements are absolute and some have been invented by humans.

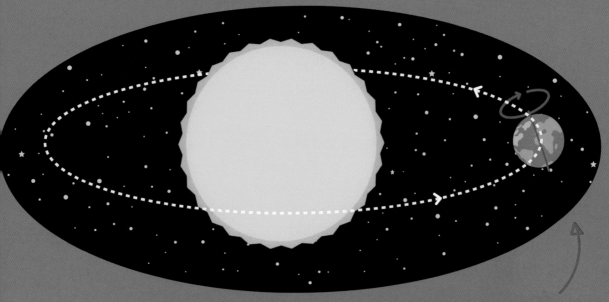

The Earth always takes one year to orbit the Sun and always takes one day to spin on its axis. These are absolute measurements.

Humans decided to divide the day into 24 hours.

A different way of dividing the day could have been chosen—imagine if we only had three hours in a day!

Strange measurements
... in 30 seconds

There are measurements that we use a lot, such as feet and pounds, and then there are less common measurements. There are different—and very odd—units of measurement for special things.

Jewels are small, but very precious. They have been valuable for a long time—long before we had pounds as a unit of weight. Jewels are still measured in "carats." A carat is the weight of a carob seed. Carob seeds are quite regular in size, so jewel-merchants in ancient times used them as a measurement of weight.

The brightness of stars is measured by "magnitude." The higher the number, the dimmer the star. Most people can't see stars of magnitude more than 6 without using a telescope.

The heat of chili peppers is measured using the Scoville Heat Scale. This measures the amount of a super-hot spicy chemical they contain. A pimiento pepper scores 100—500, but pure chili extract can score 16 million!

There are measurements for how clear seawater is, for how much something hurts, and for how hard rocks are. Some things are very hard to measure. We measure how explosive a volcano is by calculating how much scorching rock, dust, and gas comes from it.

3-second sum-up

Certain things are measured using special scales.

3-minute mission Invent a measurement

You need: • Paper • Markers or colored pencils

Make up your own scale to measure something—maybe how difficult your homework is, how sweet a cake is, how annoying your parents are being, or how smelly something is. Invent a unit of measurement and set up a scale. Draw a chart to show the different ratings.

Some measurements are very common, but people have also created lots of other, more unusual measurements.

Jewels are measured in units called carats, an ancient word for "carob seed." This measurement has been used for thousands of years.

Measuring the heat of different varieties of chili peppers tells us which we can eat and which we can't.

A scale called the Volcanic Explosivity Index measures volcanic eruptions.

Measuring and calculating

... in 30 seconds

It's easy to measure the length of your bedroom or the height of the table. But some things are much trickier to measure. What if you wanted to know how tall a tree in the park is, or how much water is in a pond? You can't climb to the top of a tree with a tape measure or empty the pond into a lot of buckets. Sometimes we have to calculate instead.

To figure out how much water is in a rectangular pond, you would need to measure its sides and its depth, and then do this calculation to find its volume:

LENGTH of the pond × WIDTH of the pond × DEPTH of the pond = VOLUME.

If you've measured the pond in feet, this calculates the volume in "cubic feet." One cubic foot is about 7.5 gallons.

You don't always need special measuring tools, such as a ruler or measuring cup, to measure things. You can use something else and then measure that later. This is useful if you want to measure wiggly or irregular things. For instance, you could use a piece of string to measure a worm and then use a ruler to measure the string.

3-second sum-up

Some things are hard to measure directly, so we use calculations instead.

3-minute mission Measure your head

You will need: • String • Scissors • Ruler

Hold one end of the string on the bridge of your nose between your eyes. Loop the string around your head and back to your nose. Pinch the point on the string where it meets the first end. Take it off your head and either cut or tie a knot in the string. Then measure it using the ruler to find the distance around your head.

If you can't measure something directly, you can often figure out its size. You can do this by measuring something else and then using that measurement in a calculation.

You can use your shadow to roughly work out the height of a tree.

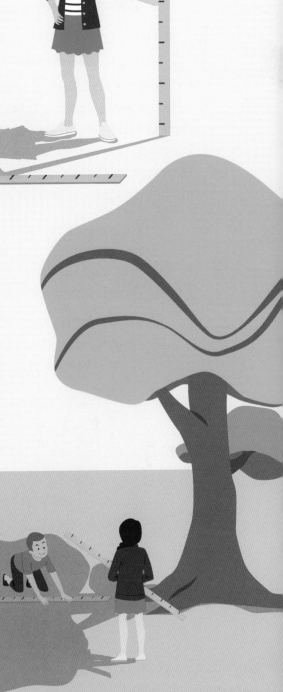

On a sunny day, measure your height and measure the length of your shadow in inches. Divide your height by the length of your shadow.

$$\frac{\text{Height}}{\text{Shadow}} = \frac{60}{40} = \frac{3}{2} = 1.5$$

Then, making sure it's the same time of day, measure the shadow of the tree. Multiply the length of the tree's shadow by the proportion you've just calculated.

For example:
Tree's shadow = 10 ft
10 ft × 1.5 = 15 ft
So the tree would be roughly 15 ft tall.

Double the size

... in 30 seconds

It's easy to see if one ice-cream cone is bigger than another—but can you tell how much bigger? Describing relative sizes can be tricky.

Imagine a school has a playground 100 ft by 100 ft. Another school has a playground with sides twice as long—200 ft by 200 ft. In other words, it's twice the size—right? Well, let's calculate the area of each playground and see. The smaller playground measures 100 ft × 100 ft = 10,000 square feet (ft^2). The bigger playground measures 200 ft × 200 ft = 40,000 square feet (ft^2)—that's actually four times the size of the smaller one!

Volumes are even more interesting. If you had a cube with sides measuring 2 in, you might think you could double its size by making each side 4 in. But, in fact, this would give a cube with eight times the volume (2 × 2 × 2), as you'll have doubled each dimension!

Knowing this helps you to spot a good deal—or a bad deal. If a pizza parlor sells pizzas that are 8 in or 12 in across, the bigger one isn't just 1.5 times bigger—it's more than twice the size!

3-second sum-up

Doubling the length of a shape's sides makes it bigger than double the size.

3-minute mission Prove it!

You will need: • Tray of ice cubes • Measuring cup

Take nine ice cubes out of the tray. Put one on its own and arrange the others in a cube-shaped pile, 2 × 2 × 2. You can easily see that doubling the length of the sides means you use eight times as many ice cubes. Melt the single ice cube in the cup and measure the volume. Now throw that away, melt the other eight in the cup, and check the volume of water.

When you double the length of a shape's sides, its area is multiplied by four and its volume is multiplied by eight.

A playground has four times as much area, or space to play, if you double the length of each of its sides.

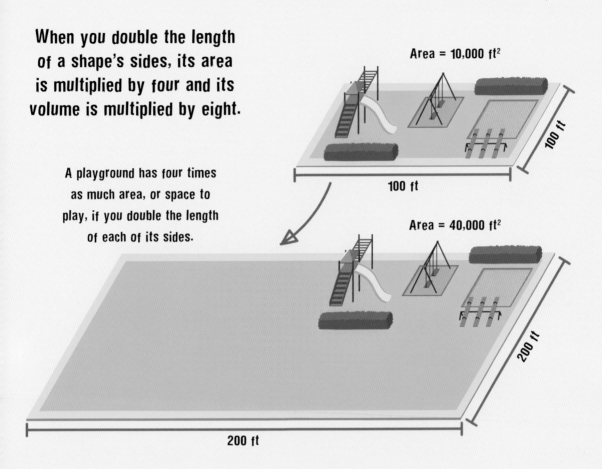

Area = 10,000 ft²

100 ft

100 ft

Area = 40,000 ft²

200 ft

200 ft

If you can keep two fish in a small aquarium, doubling the length of each side would mean you could keep eight times as many fish—so sixteen!

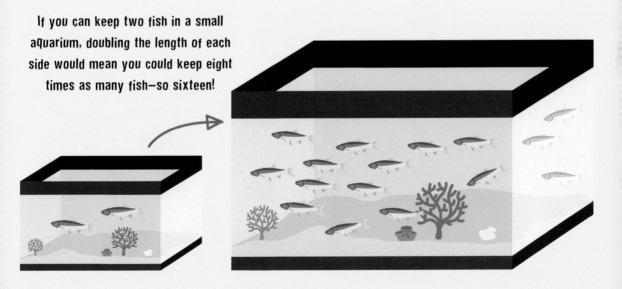

A date with data

A big list of numbers can be hard to understand. Luckily, there are better ways of showing mathematical information, such as in graphs and charts or by grouping things in sets. When looked at in the right way, data (number information) can be really useful for describing and understanding the world around us and for making predictions about what might happen in the future. You could use data to find out how many people in the country have a pet, or how tall a puppy is likely to grow.

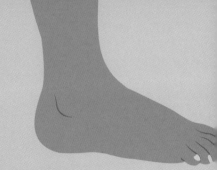

A date with data
Glossary

average The **calculated** middle or typical **value** of a set of numbers. There are several types of average.

bar chart A way of presenting **data** using rectangular bars to show quantities.

calculate To figure out using mathematical operations (adding, subtracting, multiplying, and dividing).

compare To look for similarity or difference between two or more items or **sets**.

data A collection of facts and figures, often text and numbers.

estimate To do a rough **calculation** that gives you a **value** close enough to the right answer.

fraction Only part of a whole item or number. Fractions are helpful for counting and **measuring** between whole numbers and for splitting things into **portions** or groups. Examples of fractions include ½ and ¾.

line graph A way of presenting **data** using points connected with lines to show changing quantities.

measure To find out size or quantity. You can measure all sorts of things, including distance, weight, volume, time, or temperature.

percentage A **proportion** expressed as part of 100. For example, 50 percent means 50 out of 100. Percentages are often used to show **probabilities**.

pictogram A way of presenting **data** using pictures or symbols to show quantities.

pie chart A way of presenting information using a circle divided into sections. The circle represents the whole **sample** and each section shows a **proportion** of the total.

portion A part of a whole.

probability The chance that something will happen (a possible outcome), normally shown as a **percentage** or a **fraction**.

proportion The number or size of a part of something in relation to the whole thing.

range The spread of **values**, between the highest and lowest in a **set**.

sample A section of a whole group. When you conduct a **survey**, the sample is the group of people who answer the questions.

set A collection of items. The items could be anything, including animals, numbers, or types of food.

subset A smaller group, within a larger **set**.

survey A way of collecting **data** by asking people questions.

value An amount, or how much something is worth.

Venn diagram A way of presenting information using overlapping circles to show the relationship between different **sets**.

Showing data

... in 30 seconds

You've probably seen and heard reports such as "one in ten people is vegetarian" or "50% of families have a pet." This information is gathered by researchers asking people questions, or measuring things. The researchers can then make graphs and charts to show the results clearly.

Different types of charts suit different data. Pictograms and bar charts are good for data that falls into clear categories. For example, it's easy to compare how many people have different types of pets using these kinds of charts.

If you want to record the growth of a sunflower, a line graph would be the best way. The plant grows all the time—it doesn't suddenly jump from 4 ft to 5 ft—and the graph shows this. You can even estimate its height on days when you didn't measure it.

A pie chart is good for showing how a group is divided. You could draw a pie chart to show which flavors of pie people like best! The size of each portion of the chart would reflect the popularity of each flavor.

3-second sum-up

Different types of graphs work for different types of data.

3-minute mission Make a pictogram

You will need: • Friends • Pencil • Paper

Choose a question that has roughly five answers to ask your friends. You could ask how they travel to school, what type of pet they have, or which sport they like best. Count how many people give each answer. Draw a pictogram to show your results using icons (small pictures) for each column.

Pictograms and bar charts are perfect for showing data that falls into clear categories, line graphs are good for showing how something changes over time, and pie charts show how something is divided.

It's easy to see from a pictogram or bar chart how many people have each type of pet.

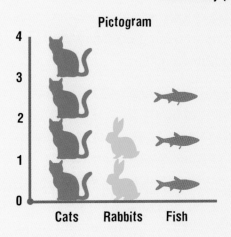

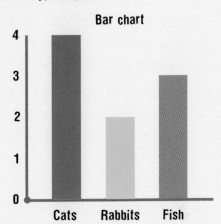

Even though the sunflower is only measured at certain points, a line graph shows how it grows continuously over time.

A pie chart clearly shows the proportion of people in a group who like a particular type of pie.

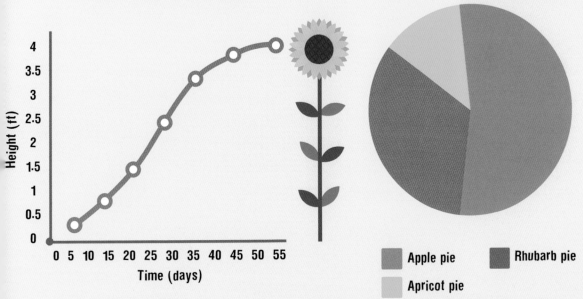

Surveys and samples

... in 30 seconds

Surveys are a way of collecting data by asking people questions. You can't usually ask everyone who might be affected by a question. You might ask everyone in your class what pets they have, but you probably wouldn't ask the whole school and you certainly couldn't ask everyone in the country! The people you ask are called the sample.

It's easier to grasp the meaning of "a quarter of people like bananas" or "25% of people like bananas" than it is to figure out "32 out of 128 people said they like bananas." For this reason, the results of a study or survey are often given as a fraction or a percentage. This clearly shows the proportion of the sample that gave a particular answer.

You can apply the answers from your smaller sample to a larger group if you choose the sample fairly. So if you found that a third of the children in your class have a dog, you could reasonably assume that about a third of children in the school have a dog. If there are 900 children in the school, that means that about 300 have a dog. This is called "scaling up" from a sample.

3-second sum-up

Surveys and samples provide data that we can apply to larger populations or studies.

3-minute mission Favorite stories

A newspaper report on a study of 100 children found that:

"Half the children like to read adventure stories; two out of five said they prefer funny stories; ten percent preferred animal stories."

Can you figure out how many children liked:

(a) adventure stories?

(b) funny stories?

(c) animal stories?

Answers on page 96

Data from a sample can be scaled up and then used to figure out proportions for a larger group.

In a sample of 10 people, 4 have cats and 6 don't. So, in a group of 30 people, you can assume that 12 would have cats and 18 wouldn't.

$^4/_{10}$ is the same as $^{12}/_{30}$

Samples and proportions aren't only limited to surveys. One bone is a sample of a whole dinosaur. Scientists can often figure out an animal's approximate size from a single bone.

25 ft

47 in

20 ft

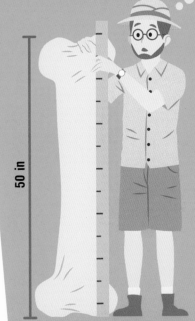

50 in

So if a dinosaur that was 20 ft tall had a leg bone that was 50 in long, we could assume that a dinosaur with a leg bone of 60 in would be roughly 25 ft tall.

20 ft ÷ 50 in = 4.8
60 in × 5 = 300 in

Averages and ranges

... in 30 seconds

Figuring out an average gives you a "typical" value for a set of data. There are three different types of average: the mean, the mode, and the median. You can find the mean of a set of data by adding all the numbers together and dividing the total by how many numbers there are in the set. The mode is the most common number in a set and the median is the value in the middle of a set if the numbers are put in order from smallest to largest.

Imagine you are thinking of getting a puppy. It would be good to know roughly how big your dog will be when it grows up. To find out, you could figure out the mean height of a particular breed of dog. Add up the heights of a group of the dogs and divide the total by the number of dogs in the group

For example, if six Dalmatians are 53 in, 54 in, 61 in, 63 in, 64 in, and 65 in, the mean is:

$$53 + 54 + 61 + 63 + 64 + 65 = 360$$

$$360 \div 6 = 60 \text{ in.}$$

It's also useful to see the range of values. What's the biggest your dog might grow? The range is set by the lowest and highest values. From this sample, you wouldn't expect your dog to be smaller than 53 in or larger than 65 in.

3-second sum-up

Range and averages help us understand the patterns and information in a set of data.

3-minute mission Big feet, little feet

You need: • Ruler • Paper • Pencil • Calculator • Friends or family

Measure the feet of your friends or family. Make sure you measure the same foot (left or right) for everyone. What is the range of foot sizes? Whose is biggest and whose is smallest? What is the mean (average) foot size? Does anyone have the average-size foot?

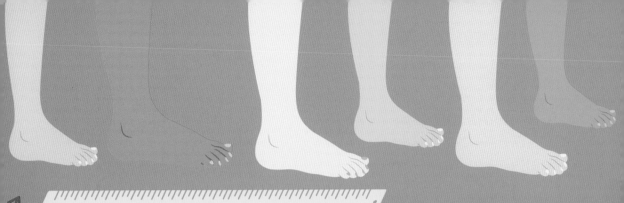

An average value is a good representation of a set of data. The range of values is the difference between the smallest and the largest values.

If you wanted to figure out the average foot size in your school, you would need to measure a lot of feet. If you could only measure a sample, a larger sample would give better results.

Knowing the average size of a fully grown dog could help you decide what size kennel or bed to buy for a puppy.

65 in

60 in

55 in

50 in

45 in

40 in

Sets

... in 30 seconds

You're probably used to the idea of sets already. A set is a group of things that have something in common. We use sets in math, too. They're a way of doing math without using any numbers!

One big set of common things is called a "universal" set. For example, a universal set of animals would include every type of animal. "Subsets" are divisions of the universal set. Subsets could be different types of animals, such as mammals, birds, and reptiles, or "animals that have wings" and "animals that go in water."

Often, items can be in more than one set. For example, ducks have wings and also go in water. But some sets have no overlaps—for example, an animal can't be both a reptile and a mammal.

Sets are drawn as circles in a special type of picture called a Venn diagram. The circles overlap if any items can be in both sets.

We can compare sets and see if they are equal. For example, the sets "has feathers" and "is a bird" have exactly the same animals in them: the two sets are equal since all birds have feathers and all animals with feathers are birds.

3-second sum-up

Sets give us a way of showing and comparing groups without using numbers.

3-minute mission Setting up sets

You need: • Family, friends, or class • Paper • Markers or colored pencils • Compasses

Use your family, group of friends, or class as a universal set. Choose subsets to divide them into. For example, it could be sets such as "has dark hair" or "likes fruit" or "enjoys swimming." Draw a Venn diagram showing how some of the sets overlap.

Venn diagrams show us sets and subsets so that we can identify similarities and differences.

animals	reptiles

The set of "reptiles" is a subset of "animals"—all reptiles are animals, but not all animals are reptiles.

has wings	goes in water

Birds can belong to either or both sets "has wings" and "goes in the water." The animals that belong to both sets are in the overlapping area.

animals with two legs

animals with four legs

These sets don't overlap— an animal can't have four legs and also have only two legs.

eats plants

goes in water

has wings

The sets here overlap. One animal belongs in all three sets.

What are the chances?

Life is full of chances and risks, dangers and opportunities. Math gives us ways of figuring out which chances are worth taking and which aren't. But even with lots of math, life can still surprise you! We can often figure out the chance of something happening, but we can hardly ever be certain. Something unexpected can always come along!

What are the chances?
Glossary

decimal number A type of **fraction** that breaks numbers down into tenths, hundredths, thousandths, and so on. The whole number is separated from the fraction with a decimal point. Examples of decimal numbers include 0.1 and 2.5.

calculate To figure out using mathematical operations (adding, subtracting, multiplying, and dividing).

equation A mathematical sum that shows two things that are equal.

fraction Only part of a whole item or number. Fractions are helpful for counting and measuring between whole numbers and for splitting things into portions or groups. Examples of fractions include ½ and ¾.

outcome A result.

probability The chance that something will happen (a possible **outcome**), normally shown as a percentage or a **fraction**.

risk The possibility of a negative **outcome**.

variables Things that can change.

Probability

... in 30 seconds

If you toss a coin, it can come down facing head or tail side up—these are the only two possibilities (possible outcomes). On average, the coin will land "heads" half the time and "tails" half the time. The chance of a particular outcome happening is called the probability.

We write probabilities as fractions or decimals:

Heads: ½ (0.5)   **Tails:** ½ (0.5)

The probabilities always add up to 1: ½ (0.5) + ½ (0.5) = 1.

If you toss two coins, each one could come down heads or tails. Since there are two coins, there are four possible outcomes.

The probability of both coins coming down heads side up is ¼.

The probability of one coin coming down heads and one coming down tails is ¼ + ¼ = ½, since there are two ways that this could happen.

Coin 1	Coin 2
Heads	Heads
Heads	Tails
Tails	Heads
Tails	Tails

To find the probability of two or more outcomes, you multiply the probabilities, so, if you're tossing just one coin, the probability of it coming down heads twice in a row is ½ × ½ = ¼.

3-second sum-up

Probabilities express the chance of something happening, shown as a decimal or fraction.

3-minute mission Rock, paper, scissors

You need: • A friend

In the game "rock, paper, scissors," two players shout or make a sign meaning "rock," "paper," or "scissors" at the same time. Play it with a friend, noting down your choices for 20 turns. How many times did you make the same choice? The probability each time is ⅓.

Probabilities are all around us—you can use them to figure out the chance of almost any future event.

The probability of the bird landing on a black stripe is $\frac{4}{8} = \frac{1}{2}$.

The probability of getting the chocolate cookie improves each time someone takes a plain one.

If there are 10 cookies, the probability is $\frac{1}{10}$ for the first person who takes a cookie, $\frac{1}{9}$ for the second, and so on, until someone takes the chocolate cookie.

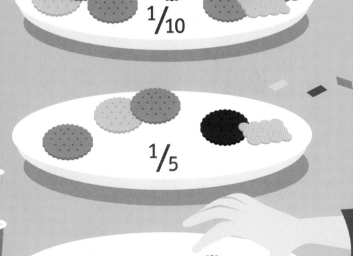

$\frac{1}{10}$

$\frac{1}{5}$

$\frac{1}{2}$

Good risk, bad risk

... in 30 seconds

It's great to know the probability of something happening—
but what will you do with the information?

The way we respond to probabilities depends very much on how
good or bad the outcome might be. If you thought there was a
$\frac{1}{10}$ probability (a 1-in-10 chance) that you would break your leg
doing a dangerous but fun stunt, you probably wouldn't do the
stunt. But if there was a $\frac{1}{10}$ probability that you would get a
scraped knee, you might think it was worth the risk.

We make the same calculation when there is a chance of a good
outcome. You would be more likely to put a lot of time into a
competition that gave you a $\frac{1}{100}$ probability (1-in-100 chance)
of winning a new bike than one that gave you a $\frac{1}{100}$ probability
of winning a bike helmet. The bigger the prize, the more likely
we are to take the chance. That's why so many people buy lottery
tickets, even though the chance of winning is often less than
one in a million.

3-second sum-up

People don't only
consider numbers
when thinking
about chances,
they look at the
consequences, too.

The bigger the number...

Research has found we're attracted to large numbers. If people
are asked to choose between a grab bag that has nine losing
tickets and one winning ticket, and a grab bag that has eight
winning tickets and 92 losing tickets, most people choose the
second. But it offers a lower chance of winning—8-in-100
instead of 10-in-100.

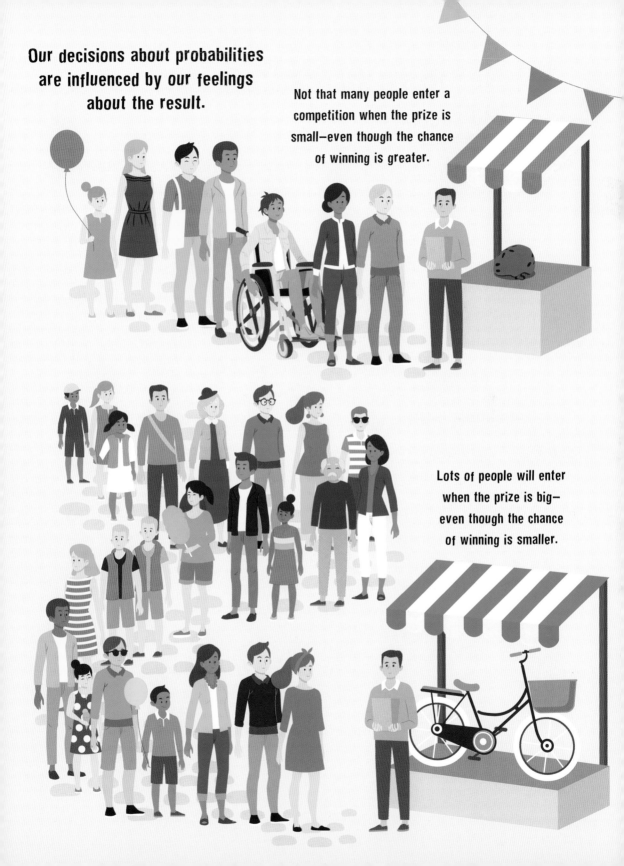

Our decisions about probabilities are influenced by our feelings about the result.

Not that many people enter a competition when the prize is small—even though the chance of winning is greater.

Lots of people will enter when the prize is big—even though the chance of winning is smaller.

Impossible probabilities

... in 30 seconds

What's the probability that you will live to 100? What's the probability that humans will communicate with aliens in the future? We can't really say.

Sometimes it's impossible to figure out a probability because there are too many variables (things that can change). How long you will live depends on your lifestyle, but also on a lot of unpredictable events.

The Drake equation was invented as a way of figuring out the probability of humans contacting aliens. It tells us to multiply:

- the average rate at which stars form
- the fraction of stars with planets
- the average number of planets that could support life
- the fraction of planets that develop life
- the fraction of planets with life that have civilizations
- the fraction of civilizations that send (or leak) signals into space
- how long they release signals for.

The problem is, we don't know the numbers to use. If we guess, answers come out between hardly any alien civilizations, and millions of them!

100

3-second sum-up

Just because we know how to figure out a probability, doesn't mean we can actually do it!

And when is "now?"

Places in space are a long way apart. One exoplanet (a planet that orbits a star outside of our solar system) that is quite like Earth is 1,400 light-years away. So if we did find a signal, it would have been sent 1,400 years ago. Our reply would take 1,400 years to get back to them, too. After 2,800 years, the aliens might have given up waiting.

Often we can't figure out the probability of certain things happening in life since there are just too many variables to take into account.

Sell your paintings in a local gallery?

Go to art classes

Go to space and meet an alien?

Study space

Paint a celebrity's portrait?

Become an astronomer?

Become a marine biologist?

Break your leg while playing a game?

Practice soccer

Learn to scuba dive

Play for your local team and win a trophy?

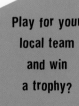

Discover long-lost shipwreck and treasure?

Discover more

NONFICTION BOOKS

50 Amazing Things Kids Need to Know About Math by Anne Rooney
Sky Pony Press, 2012

Go Figure! Math Journey series titles by Hillary Koll, Steve Mills, Anne Rooney
Crabtree, 2014–17

Maths is Everywhere: Super Sums by Rob Colson
Franklin Watts, 2016

Maths is Everywhere: Get the Measure by Rob Colson
Franklin Watts, 2016

Mathmagicians by Johnny Ball
DK Children's, 2016

Think of a Number by Johnny Ball
DK Children's, 2010

This is Not a Math Book by Anna Weltman
Ivy Kids, 2015

FICTION BOOKS

The Number Devil by Hans Magnus Enzensberger
Picador, 2010

Fractions in Disguise by Edward Einhorn
Charlesbridge Publishing, 2014

APPS

Zoombinis by Broderbund Software
Apple iOS, Android, Kindle

10 Minutes a Day Times Tables by Dorling Kindersley
Apple iOS, Android

WEBSITES

Mathcats
http://www.mathcats.com/explore.html

Mathplayground
http://www.mathplayground.com/

Cool Math Games
http://www.coolmath.com/0-cool-math-games-and-problems

ONLINE DOCUMENTARIES

National Geographic: Decoding the Universe, The Great Math Mystery
National Geographic, 2015

National Geographic: My Brilliant Brain
National Geographic, 2010

Although every endeavor has been made by the publisher to
ensure that all content from these websites is educational material
of the highest quality and is age appropriate, we strongly advise
that Internet access is supervised by a responsible adult.

Index

Answers

Page 32 Surface area and speed

The loose sugar will dissolve fastest because it has a higher surface-area-to-volume ratio.

Page 62 Your body in numbers

Height—feet

Around your waist, around your wrist, and the length of your leg—all inches

A hair from your head—inches

Your nose and across your smallest fingernail—fractions of inches

Page 76 Favorite stories

(a) 50 (b) 40 (c) 10